STARTING SMALL
WINNING BIG

The Journey of an Entrepreneur Without Capital

By Sharon Mathew

Chapter 1:

Introduction

The challenges of being an entrepreneur without startup capital: This section will outline some of the common difficulties faced by entrepreneurs who don't have access to significant startup funds, such as limited resources, difficulty attracting investors, and heightened financial risk.

The importance of mindset and determination: This section will discuss the importance of a positive and resilient mindset for entrepreneurs on a tight budget. It will also provide some tips for developing a strong entrepreneurial mindset, such as focusing on the long-term vision, being adaptable, and staying motivated in the face of challenges.

Entrepreneurs who don't have access to significant startup funds face a number of common difficulties, including:

- Limited resources: Without startup capital, entrepreneurs may struggle to secure office space, equipment, and other essential resources. They may also have limited access to professional services like legal or accounting support.
- Difficulty attracting investors: Investors are often hesitant to invest in businesses without a proven track record or significant capital backing. This can make it difficult for entrepreneurs without startup funds to secure the funding they need to launch or grow their business.
- Heightened financial risk: Starting a business without capital often means assuming significant financial risk. Entrepreneurs may need to invest their own savings, rely on credit cards or loans with high interest rates, or work longer hours without a guaranteed paycheck.
- Limited marketing and advertising: Marketing and advertising can be expensive, which can be a major obstacle for entrepreneurs on a tight budget. Without significant funds, it may be challenging to reach potential customers and build brand recognition.
- Time constraints: Entrepreneurs without startup capital often need to juggle multiple responsibilities, such as working a day job to make ends meet while also trying to launch and grow their business. This can make it difficult to find the time and energy needed to devote to their business.

These challenges can be daunting, but they are not insurmountable.

The importance of mindset and determination cannot be overstated when it comes to being an entrepreneur on a tight budget. Building and maintaining a positive and resilient mindset can help entrepreneurs overcome obstacles, stay motivated, and achieve their goals. Here are some tips for developing a strong entrepreneurial mindset:

- Focus on the long-term vision: When you're working with limited resources and facing significant challenges, it can be easy to get bogged down in the day-to-day details. However, it's important to keep your long-term vision in mind and stay focused on your ultimate goals. This can help you stay motivated and make strategic decisions that will benefit your business in the long run.
- Be adaptable: Entrepreneurs without startup capital often need to be creative and adaptable in order to succeed. Being willing to pivot, adjust your approach, and try new things can help you stay nimble and responsive to changing circumstances.
- Stay motivated in the face of challenges: Starting a business without capital is not easy, and there will be many challenges along the way. It's important to stay motivated and focused, even when things get tough. This might involve setting specific goals, finding inspiration from other successful entrepreneurs, or building a supportive community of peers and mentors.

- Embrace a growth mindset: A growth mindset involves embracing challenges, learning from failure, and continuously improving. Entrepreneurs without startup capital can benefit from cultivating a growth mindset, as it can help them approach challenges as opportunities for growth and learning.

Recognize that success is not just a matter of having access to capital, but also of cultivating the right mindset and attitude. By providing practical tips for developing a strong entrepreneurial mindset, you can empower your readers to overcome obstacles and achieve their goals, even in the face of significant challenges.

This eBook is designed to help entrepreneurs who don't have access to significant startup capital navigate the challenges of building a business on a tight budget. In the first chapter, we discussed the importance of mindset and determination for entrepreneurs facing these challenges. In subsequent chapters, we'll explore specific strategies and tactics for identifying opportunities, bootstrapping your business, building a strong online presence, creating effective marketing and sales strategies, building a supportive community, and staying motivated in the face of obstacles. By the end of the eBook, readers should have a range of practical tools and insights for building a successful business without breaking the bank.

Chapter 2: Finding Your Niche

One of the keys to building a successful business on a tight budget is finding a profitable niche market. In this chapter, we'll discuss how to identify a niche that is both profitable and aligned with your skills and interests. We'll explore strategies for researching and selecting a niche that is likely to generate revenue and sustain your business over the long-term.

Identifying a profitable niche market requires a deep understanding of your target audience, their needs, and the competitive landscape. We'll discuss how to conduct market research to identify gaps in the market and evaluate the potential demand for your products or services. We'll also explore the importance of identifying a niche that aligns with your own skills and interests, as this can help you differentiate your business and maintain a strong sense of passion and purpose.

Once you have identified a potential niche, we'll explore strategies for testing and validating your assumptions. This can help you ensure that there is sufficient demand for your products or services before you invest significant time and resources into developing your business. We'll also discuss how to evaluate the competitive landscape and identify opportunities to differentiate your business from others in the market.

By the end of this chapter, you should have a clear understanding of how to identify a profitable niche market and strategies for researching and selecting a niche that is aligned with your skills, interests, and budget. This will lay the foundation for the subsequent chapters on bootstrapping, marketing, and building a strong online presence.

When it comes to identifying a niche that is both profitable and aligned with your skills and interests, there are several strategies that entrepreneurs can use to research and select a niche that is likely to generate revenue and sustain their business over the long-term:

- Evaluate your skills and interests: Start by making a list of your skills, passions, and interests. This will help you identify potential niches that align with your strengths and personal preferences.
- Conduct market research: Once you have a list of potential niches, conduct market research to evaluate the demand and potential profitability of each niche. You can use online tools like Google

Trends, social media analytics, and keyword research to identify popular topics and potential niches.

- Identify gaps in the market: Look for gaps in the market where there is high demand but low competition. This can help you identify niches that are likely to be profitable and sustain your business over the long-term.
- Evaluate the competition: Assess the competition in each niche and look for opportunities to differentiate your business from others in the market. This can help you stand out and attract customers who are looking for something unique.
- Consider the revenue potential: Evaluate the revenue potential of each niche and consider factors like pricing, market size, and profit margins. This can help you identify niches that are likely to generate sustainable revenue and support your business over the long-term.

By using these strategies to identify a niche that is both profitable and aligned with your skills and interests, entrepreneurs can increase their chances of building a successful business on a tight budget. It's important to conduct thorough research and carefully evaluate potential niches before investing significant time and resources into developing your business.

Conducting market research is crucial for identifying gaps in the market and evaluating the potential demand for your products or services. Here are some steps to follow when conducting market research:

- Identify your target audience: Begin by identifying your target audience and understanding their needs and pain points. This can help you identify potential niches that align with their needs.

- Evaluate the competition: Assess the competition in each niche and look for opportunities to differentiate your business from others in the market. This can help you stand out and attract customers who are looking for something unique.
- Conduct customer interviews: Reach out to potential customers and conduct interviews to gather feedback on their needs and preferences. This can help you identify gaps in the market and validate your assumptions about potential niches.
- Use online tools: Use online tools like Google Trends, social media analytics, and keyword research to identify popular topics and potential niches. These tools can help you gauge the potential demand for your products or services.

It's also important to identify a niche that aligns with your own skills and interests. This can help you differentiate your business and maintain a strong sense of passion and purpose. When you're passionate about your business, you're more likely to stay motivated and committed over the long-term.

By conducting thorough market research and identifying a niche that aligns with your skills and interests, you can increase your chances of building a successful business on a tight budget. Remember to evaluate the potential demand for your products or services and look for gaps in the market where you can differentiate your business and stand out from the competition.

Testing and validating assumptions:

- Conduct Market Research: Conduct market research to gather insights about your target audience, including their needs, wants, preferences, and behaviors. You can use online surveys, focus groups, interviews, and observation to gather data. This will help you understand whether there is sufficient demand for your products or services before investing significant time and resources into developing your business.
- Create a Minimum Viable Product (MVP): Develop a minimum viable product that showcases your product or service's core features and functionalities. This will help you test your assumptions and gather feedback from potential customers before investing more resources.
- Test Your MVP: Test your MVP with a small group of potential customers to gather feedback and identify any flaws or areas of improvement. This will help you validate your assumptions and ensure that you are on the right track.
- Analyze Feedback: Analyze the feedback you receive from potential customers and adjust your product or service accordingly. This will help you ensure that you are meeting the needs and wants of your target audience.

Evaluating the competitive landscape:

- Identify Competitors: Identify your competitors and analyze their strengths and weaknesses. This will help you understand the market and identify opportunities to differentiate your business.

- Analyze Market Trends: Analyze market trends and identify any ps or opportunities in the market. This will help you identify areas where you can differentiate your business and offer unique value to your customers.
- Conduct SWOT Analysis: Conduct a SWOT analysis (strengths, weaknesses, opportunities, threats) to identify your own strengths and weaknesses and opportunities and threats in the market. This will help you identify areas where you can differentiate your business and offer unique value to your customers.
- Differentiate Your Business: Use the insights gathered from your market research and competitive analysis to differentiate your business from others in the market. This could involve offering unique features or services, targeting a specific niche audience, or using innovative marketing strategies.
- Keep Learning: Keep learning and adapting as the market evolves. Stay up-to-date with industry news and trends, and continue to gather feedback from your customers to ensure that you are offering the best possible product or service.

To identify a profitable niche market that aligns with your skills, interests, and budget, it's important to conduct thorough market research to identify gaps or opportunities. Once you've identified your target audience and evaluated the competition, use keyword research, social media, conferences, and surveys to gather insights and validate your assumptions. To lay the foundation for subsequent chapters on bootstrapping, marketing, and building a strong online presence, consider developing a minimum viable product and testing it with potential customers. Then, use bootstrapping strategies to start and grow your business without external funding, develop a marketing strategy that aligns with your niche and target audience, and build a strong online presence with a website, social media profiles, and optimized content.

Chapter 3: Building Your Brand

Your brand is more than just your business name and logo. It's the reputation and image that you create in the minds of your customers. Building a strong brand is essential for establishing credibility and attracting customers. In this chapter, we'll discuss the importance of branding and provide tips for creating a strong brand on a tight budget.

The Importance of Branding:

A strong brand can differentiate your business from competitors, increase customer loyalty, and establish credibility. A well-crafted brand communicates your values, mission, and personality, and resonates with your target audience. It also creates an emotional connection with your customers, making them more likely to remember and recommend your business.

Creating a Strong Brand on a Tight Budget

Creating a strong brand doesn't have to be expensive. Here are some tips for building your brand on a tight **budget:**

- Define Your Brand: Start by defining your brand's values, mission, and personality. This will help you create a consistent message across all your marketing channels. Consider your target audience and what they value most.
- Create a Unique Logo: A logo is the face of your brand and can help you stand out from the competition. Create a simple and memorable logo that reflects your brand's values and personality. Use online tools like Canva or Fiverr to create a logo on a tight budget.
- Develop Your Brand Voice: Your brand voice is the tone and style of your communication. It should be consistent across all your marketing channels, including your website, social media, and email marketing. Choose a voice that resonates with your target audience.
- Use Consistent Branding: Use consistent branding across all your marketing channels, including your website, social media, and business cards. This includes your logo, brand colors, and fonts. Consistency is key to building brand recognition and trust.
- Leverage Social Media: Social media is a powerful tool for building your brand on a tight budget. Choose the platforms that your target audience uses the most and create a consistent message across all your social media channels. Engage with your audience and respond to their comments and questions.
- Collaborate with Others: Collaborating with other businesses or influencers can help you reach a wider audience and build credibility. Look for opportunities to collaborate with businesses or individuals that share your values and target audience.

- Business Description: This section provides a detailed description of your business, including your industry, market size, competition, and unique selling proposition. It should highlight your strengths and competitive advantage.
- Market Analysis: This section provides an analysis of your target market, including their needs, preferences, and behaviors. It should also analyze the competition and identify opportunities for growth.
- Products or Services: This section provides a detailed description of your products or services, including features, benefits, and pricing. It should also highlight any unique features or intellectual property.
- Marketing and Sales: This section outlines your marketing and sales strategies, including target audience, channels, and messaging. It should also include sales projections and customer acquisition costs.
- Operations and Management: This section outlines your business operations and management structure, including personnel, facilities, and technology. It should also include any legal or regulatory requirements.
- Financial Projections: This section provides detailed financial projections, including revenue, expenses, profit margins, and cash flow. It should also include funding requirements and sources of funding.

Strategies for Creating a Business Plan without Significant Capital

Creating a business plan doesn't have to be expensive. Here are some strategies for creating a business plan without significant **capital:**

- Use Online Templates: Online templates can provide a starting point for creating a business plan. There are many free templates available online, such as those provided by the Small Business Administration (SBA).
- Conduct Market Research: Conducting market research can provide valuable insights into your target market and competition. This can be done using online surveys, social media, and keyword research tools.
- Use Affordable Software: There are many affordable software solutions that can help you create financial projections and analyze data. For example, QuickBooks or Wave can help you manage finances, and Google Analytics can help you track website traffic.
- Seek Help from Business Incubators or Accelerators: Business incubators or accelerators provide resources and support to startups, including assistance with creating a business plan. Many of these programs are free or low-cost.
- Consider Crowdfunding: Crowdfunding can provide a source of funding for your business and also provide validation of your product or service. Platforms like Kickstarter or Indiegogo can help you raise funds and create buzz around your business.

Conclusion

A business plan is a critical tool for any entrepreneur. It outlines your goals, strategies, and financial projections and serves as a roadmap for your business. While creating a business plan can seem daunting, it doesn't have to be expensive. Use the strategies above to create a successful business plan without significant capital. Remember to focus on the key elements of a successful business plan, including market analysis, marketing and sales strategies, and financial projections.

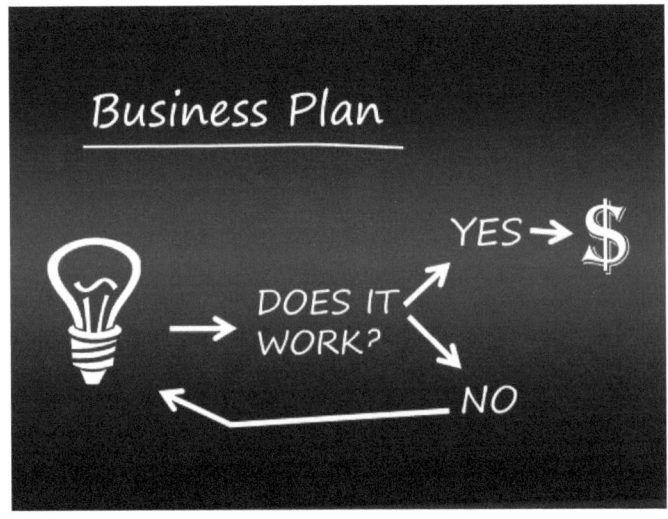

Chapter 5: Funding Your Business

Starting a business can be an exciting and rewarding endeavor, but it often requires significant upfront capital. Many entrepreneurs struggle to secure the funding they need to get their business off the ground. In this chapter, we'll explore alternative sources of funding for entrepreneurs without startup capital and provide tips for securing loans, grants, and other forms of financing.

Alternative Sources of Funding for Entrepreneurs Without Startup Capital

- Bootstrapping: Bootstrapping involves funding your business using personal savings, credit cards, or other sources of personal finance. While this can be risky, it can also give you more control over your business and increase your chances of success.
- Crowdfunding: Crowdfunding platforms like Kickstarter and Indiegogo can help entrepreneurs raise money from a large number of individual investors. This can be a great way to validate your business idea and build a community around your brand
- Small Business Loans: The Small Business Administration (SBA) provides loans to small businesses that meet certain criteria. These loans can be used for a variety of business expenses, including inventory, equipment, and working capital.
- Grants: There are many grants available to entrepreneurs, particularly those in certain industries or with specific demographics. These grants can help fund research and development, marketing, and other business expenses.

- Angel Investors: Angel investors are wealthy individuals who invest their own money in startups in exchange for a stake in the company. They can provide not only funding but also guidance and mentorship.

Tips for Securing Loans, Grants, and Other Forms of Financing

- Have a solid business plan: Having a well-crafted business plan can help demonstrate to lenders and investors that you have a viable business idea and a plan for success.
- Build a strong network: Building relationships with potential investors and lenders can help you secure funding. Attend industry events, join business organizations, and network with other entrepreneurs.
- Research your options: There are many sources of funding available, and it's important to research your options and find the best fit for your business.
- Be prepared to show financials: Lenders and investors will want to see your financial projections and revenue streams. Be prepared to provide detailed financial information to demonstrate the viability of your business.

Consider alternative forms of collateral: If you don't have sufficient collateral to secure a loan, consider alternative forms of collateral, such as inventory or accounts receivable.

Conclusion

Funding your business can be a challenging process, but it's a critical component of success. By exploring alternative sources of funding and following these tips for securing loans, grants, and other forms of financing, you can increase your chances of securing the capital you need to launch and grow your business. Remember to have a solid business plan, build a strong network, and be prepared to demonstrate the financial viability of your business. With persistence and dedication, you can find the funding you need to turn your business dreams into reality.

Chapter 6: Marketing and Sales

Marketing and sales are crucial components of any successful business, but they can also be expensive. For entrepreneurs with limited budgets, it can be challenging to find effective ways to market their business and drive sales. In this chapter, we'll explore how to effectively market your business on a shoestring budget and provide tips for driving sales and generating revenue without significant upfront costs.

How to Effectively Market Your Business on a Shoestring Budget

- Leverage social media: Social media platforms like Facebook, Twitter, and Instagram are powerful marketing tools that can help you reach a large audience for free. By creating engaging content and leveraging hashtags, you can increase your reach and build a following.

- Network with other entrepreneurs: Networking with other entrepreneurs can help you build relationships, generate referrals, and gain exposure for your business. Attend industry events, join business organizations, and participate in online communities.
- Offer free samples or trials: Offering free samples or trials of your products or services can be a powerful marketing tool that allows potential customers to experience your offerings firsthand.
- Use email marketing: Email marketing is a cost-effective way to reach a targeted audience and drive sales. By creating targeted email campaigns, you can reach out to potential customers and keep existing customers engaged.
- Focus on search engine optimization (SEO): Optimizing your website for search engines can help you attract more organic traffic and improve your visibility online. Focus on creating high-quality content and optimizing your website for relevant keywords.

Tips for Driving Sales and Generating Revenue Without Significant Upfront Costs.

- Offer discounts or promotions: Offering discounts or promotions can help drive sales and generate revenue without significant upfront costs. Consider offering a limited-time discount or running a promotion that encourages customers to make a purchase.
- Focus on upselling and cross-selling: Upselling and cross-selling can help you increase the average order value and generate more revenue from each customer. Consider offering related products or services that complement what the customer is already buying.

- Develop strategic partnerships: Developing strategic partnerships with other businesses can help you reach a new audience and generate more revenue. Consider partnering with complementary businesses in your industry or offering referral incentives to other businesses.
- Build a loyal customer base: Building a loyal customer base can help you generate repeat business and referrals. Focus on providing excellent customer service and creating a positive customer experience.
- Use data to inform your strategy: Collecting and analyzing data can help you identify areas of opportunity and improve your marketing and sales strategy. Use data to identify trends, track customer behavior, and optimize your marketing efforts.

Conclusion

Marketing and sales are critical components of any successful business, but they can also be expensive. By leveraging social media, networking with other entrepreneurs, offering free samples or trials, using email marketing, and focusing on SEO, you can effectively market your business on a shoestring budget. To drive sales and generate revenue without significant upfront costs, consider offering discounts or promotions, focusing on upselling and cross-selling, developing strategic partnerships, building a loyal customer base, and using data to inform your strategy. With persistence and dedication, you can build a successful business without breaking the bank.

Chapter 7: Building a Strong Online Presence

In today's business world, having a strong online presence is essential to success. A website and social media presence are necessary for businesses to reach their target audience, build brand awareness, and drive sales. In this chapter, we'll explore the importance of online marketing and provide strategies for building a website and leveraging social media to promote your business.T

The Importance of Online Marketing

- Reach a wider audience: With billions of people using the internet every day, having an online presence allows businesses to reach a much wider audience than traditional marketing methods.
- Build brand awareness: A strong online presence can help businesses build brand awareness by making it easy for potential customers to find them and learn more about their offerings.
- Establish credibility: A professional website and social media presence can help businesses establish credibility and make a positive impression on potential customers.
- Generate leads and drive sales: Online marketing strategies like search engine optimization (SEO), email marketing, and social media marketing can help businesses generate leads and drive sales.

Strategies for Building a Website

- Choose a domain name: A domain name is the address that people use to find your website. Choose a domain name that is easy to remember and relevant to your business.
- Select a web hosting provider: A web hosting provider is the company that stores your website and makes it available on the internet. Choose a reliable web hosting provider that offers good customer support.
- Design a website: Design a website that is visually appealing, easy to navigate, and provides visitors with the information they need to learn about your business and make a purchase.
- Optimize your website for search engines: Optimizing your website for search engines like Google can help you attract more organic traffic and improve your online visibility.
- Include a call-to-action (CTA): A CTA is a statement that encourages visitors to take a specific action, such as making a purchase or filling out a contact form. Include a clear and compelling CTA on your website to encourage visitors to take action.

Strategies for Leveraging Social Media

- Choose the right platforms: There are many social media platforms available, so it's important to choose the ones that are most relevant to your business and target audience.
- Create engaging content: Create engaging content that is relevant to your target audience and encourages engagement. This can include blog posts, videos, images, and infographics.

- Leverage hashtags: Hashtags can help increase the reach of your social media posts and make them more discoverable to a wider audience.
- Engage with your audience: Engage with your audience by responding to comments and messages, and by participating in online conversations related to your business.
- Use social media advertising: Social media advertising can be a cost-effective way to reach a targeted audience and drive sales. Consider running targeted ads on platforms like Facebook, Twitter, and LinkedIn.

Conclusion

Building a strong online presence is essential for businesses in today's digital world. By building a professional website, optimizing it for search engines, and leveraging social media to promote your business, you can reach a wider audience, build brand awareness, and drive sales. Remember to choose the right social media platforms, create engaging content, leverage hashtags, engage with your audience, and use social media advertising to achieve the best results. With dedication and persistence, you can build a strong online presence that sets your business up for success.

Chapter 8: Managing Your Finances

Managing your finances is one of the most important aspects of running a successful business. Effective cash flow management and budgeting are critical for ensuring that your business stays profitable and sustainable. In this chapter, we'll explore tips for managing cash flow and budgeting effectively, as well as strategies for minimizing expenses and maximizing profits.

Managing Cash Flow

- Track your cash flow: Keep track of your cash flow by monitoring your income and expenses on a regular basis. This will help you

identify potential cash flow problems early on and take corrective action.
- Forecast your cash flow: Use historical data to forecast your cash flow and plan for potential future expenses or revenue shortfalls.
- Manage your accounts receivable: Encourage prompt payment from customers and follow up on overdue invoices to ensure that you have a steady cash flow.
- Control your inventory: Manage your inventory carefully to ensure that you have enough products to meet demand without tying up too much cash in unsold inventory.

Budgeting Effectively

- Create a realistic budget: Create a realistic budget that takes into account all of your business expenses, including fixed costs like rent and variable costs like supplies.
- Monitor your budget: Monitor your budget on a regular basis to ensure that you are staying on track and making any necessary adjustments.
- Plan for unexpected expenses: Set aside funds for unexpected expenses, such as equipment repairs or emergency purchases.
- Prioritize expenses: Prioritize your expenses based on their importance to your business and allocate funds accordingly.
- Minimizing Expenses and Maximizing Profits
- Negotiate with vendors: Negotiate with vendors to get the best possible prices on supplies and equipment.

- Reduce overhead costs: Look for ways to reduce overhead costs, such as sharing office space or using energy-efficient equipment.
- Increase revenue: Increase revenue by exploring new revenue streams, expanding your product or service offerings, or increasing your marketing efforts.
- Focus on high-profit products or services: Focus on high-profit products or services to maximize your profits and ensure long-term sustainability.

Conclusion

Managing your finances is crucial for running a successful business. By effectively managing your cash flow, budgeting, and minimizing expenses while maximizing profits, you can ensure that your business stays profitable and sustainable. Remember to track your cash flow, create a realistic budget, prioritize expenses, negotiate with vendors, and focus on high-profit products or services. With dedication and persistence, you can build a financially stable and successful business.

Chapter 9: Building a Team

As an entrepreneur, building a team is essential to scaling your business and achieving your goals. However, hiring employees or contractors can be a costly investment, especially if you are bootstrapping your business. In this chapter, we will explore how to build a team without significant capital and provide strategies for hiring, training, and managing employees or contractors.

Building a Team without Significant Capital

- Start with part-time or contract workers: Hiring part-time or contract workers can help you manage your workload without committing to full-time salaries or benefits. You can find these workers through job boards, social media, or personal networks.
- Outsource: You can also outsource certain tasks to freelancers or contractors on a project-by-project basis, such as graphic design, content creation, or web development.
- Look for remote workers: Hiring remote workers can help you save on overhead costs, such as office space and utilities. You can find remote workers through job boards or by searching on LinkedIn for individuals with the skills you need.
- Offer equity or profit sharing: If you cannot afford to pay high salaries, consider offering equity or profit sharing to attract and retain top talent. This will give your employees or contractors a stake in the company's success, incentivizing them to work hard and contribute to your growth.
- Seek out interns or apprentices: Hiring interns or apprentices can provide you with low-cost labor while giving individuals valuable work experience. You can find interns or apprentices through universities or vocational schools.

Hiring, Training, and Managing Employees or Contractors

- Define the role: Clearly define the role and responsibilities of the position you are hiring for. This will ensure that you attract candidates with the necessary skills and experience.
- Use multiple recruitment channels: Use multiple channels to recruit candidates, such as job boards, social media, and personal networks. You can also consider partnering with recruiters or temp agencies.
- Conduct thorough interviews: Conduct thorough interviews to assess the candidate's qualifications, fit with the company culture, and overall potential. Consider asking behavioral-based interview questions to gain insight into how they handle certain situations.
- Provide comprehensive training: Once you've hired an employee or contractor, provide comprehensive training to ensure that they understand their role and responsibilities, as well as company policies and procedures.
- Set clear expectations: Set clear expectations and goals for employees or contractors, and provide regular feedback to help them improve and grow. Consider using performance metrics to track their progress and provide guidance for improvement.
- Offer professional development opportunities: Offer professional development opportunities, such as training programs or mentorship, to help employees or contractors develop new skills and advance their careers. This will not only help them grow but also benefit your business in the long run by increasing their value to your team.

Conclusion

Building a team is a crucial part of scaling your business, but it can be a costly investment. However, there are several strategies you can use to build a team without significant capital, such as hiring part-time or contract workers, outsourcing certain tasks, offering equity or profit sharing, hiring interns or apprentices, and hiring remote workers. When hiring, it's essential to define the role clearly, use multiple recruitment channels, conduct thorough interviews, provide comprehensive training, set clear expectations, and offer professional development opportunities. By following these strategies and tips, you can build a strong and effective team that will help your business achieve its goals.

Chapter 10: Conclusion

Congratulations on completing this eBook on entrepreneurship without startup capital! By now, you should have a good understanding of the strategies and tactics that can help you launch and grow a successful business, even if you don't have a lot of money to invest upfront.

Remember that while starting a business without capital can be challenging, it is also incredibly rewarding. By being scrappy and resourceful, you can build a thriving enterprise that reflects your vision and values.

Here are a few final thoughts to keep in mind as you embark on your entrepreneurial journey:

- Stay focused on your vision: Starting a business is not easy, and there will be times when you feel discouraged or overwhelmed. During those moments, it's important to remember why you started this journey in the first place.

Stay focused on your vision, and use it as a source of inspiration and motivation.

- Embrace experimentation: As an entrepreneur without startup capital, you may not have the luxury of testing every idea with expensive market research. Instead, embrace experimentation and try new things to see what works for your business. Learn from your failures, and keep moving forward.
- Seek out support: Building a business can be lonely, but you don't have to do it alone. Seek out support from friends, family, mentors, and other entrepreneurs. Join online communities, attend networking events, and connect with like-minded individuals who can provide encouragement and advice.
- Don't be afraid to pivot: As you grow your business, you may find that your original idea needs to be tweaked or even completely overhauled. Don't be afraid to pivot and make changes to your business model or product offerings if they aren't working. Being flexible and adaptable is key to long-term success.
- Celebrate your wins: Finally, remember to celebrate your wins, no matter how small they may seem. Building a business without startup capital is a significant accomplishment, and every milestone deserves recognition and celebration.
- With these tips in mind, you are well on your way to achieving your entrepreneurial dreams. Remember that success is not just about financial gain, but also about

creating something meaningful and impactful. Best of luck on your journey!

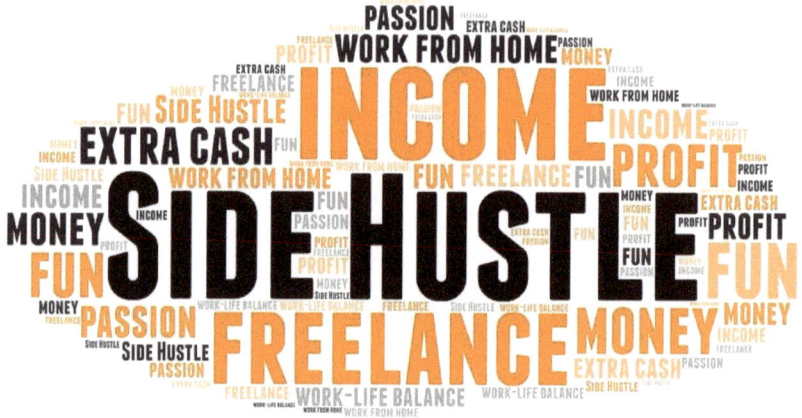

Summary

This ebook provides a comprehensive guide for entrepreneurs looking to start a business without significant startup capital. It covers various aspects of entrepreneurship, including finding a profitable niche market, building a strong brand, developing a business plan, funding options, marketing and sales strategies, building an online presence, managing finances, and building a team. The ebook emphasizes the importance of mindset, determination, and creativity when starting a business with limited resources. It also offers practical tips and strategies for minimizing expenses and maximizing profits. The ebook concludes with encouraging words and advice for those on a tight budget to pursue their entrepreneurial dreams. Overall, this ebook provides a useful resource for anyone looking to start a business on a shoestring budget.

- Sharon Mathew

www.ingramcontent.com/pod-product-compliance
Lightning Source LLC
Chambersburg PA
CBHW040400220526
45473CB00025B/2725